Learning to Make Peace in the World

Joseph N. DeLuca, MD, PhD

Strategic Book Publishing and Rights Co.

Dedication

To everyone who is eager to learn from the experiences of others to enhance their psychological health and well-being.

Acknowledgement

I wish to thank my beautiful wife Dr. Penny DeLuca for her excellent job of editing. Her continued enthusiastic support for me to write books to enhance the well-being of others is appreciated.

Introduction

The purpose of this book is to enable peace by having you develop compassion, gratitude, and forgiveness toward others. Learning the skills for peace in the world is essential for our survival.

Preparation for Goal Setting and Redreaming

* * * * *

Replay one past positive experience every day.

* * * * *

* * * * *

Think about things in the past that gave you goosebumps

* * * * *

* * * * *

If you have a dream that has been shattered, "redream" another dream.

* * * * *

Goals

Always have a dream that you are pursuing. Everyday do something that is meaningful.

* * * * *

* * * * *

It's Fun to Use Your Imagination.

* * * * *

Make a list of your goals in life and plan on how to achieve them. Look at that list every day.

* * * * *

A comfort zone is a beautiful place, but nothing ever grows there.

* * * * *

Look at the bumps in the road in your life as learning experiences.

* * * * *

All significant achievement involves some degree of pain—sorry about that!

* * * * *

Sometimes just asking for what you need will get it for you.

* * * * *

* * * * *

It is Fun to Never Ever Give Up.

* * * * *

You Need Your Health

Deep breathing exercises should be part of everyone's day.

* * * * *

Exercise increases all the neurotransmitters in your brain that enhance mood.

* * * * *

You are what you eat. Why make yourself a human garbage can?

* * * * *

Building Character to Succeed

Reputation is what others think about you. Character is what you and God know about you.

If someone says something about you that you do not like, you can always say, "it is fake information."

* * * * *

Practice being the person you want to be.

* * * * *

The world might think you are a nobody, but to somebody you are the world.

* * * * *

High school is over. It is not how good-looking you are that counts. It's how nice you are that counts.

* * * * *

If you think you're "hot stuff," try developing the courage to experience being a nobody.

* * * * *

* * * * *

Be a good listener.

* * * * *

To get in touch with pure innocence,
play with babies, puppies,
and kittens.

* * * * *

It is not what you see. It is how you interpret what you see.

* * * * *

Attitude beats aptitude.

A word, a look, a touch can change a person's life forever.

* * * * *

Snuggle with someone you love, every day.

* * * * *

Do a good deed, then quietly disappear.

* * * * *

Try and make tomorrow an improved version of what you are today.

* * * * *

Savor every moment with a loved one. You never know when that will be the very last moment you will ever have with them.

* * * * *

Getting in touch with our inner child is the key to understanding ourselves.

* * * * *

* * * * *

It takes more courage to admit to a problem, than to deny it.

* * * * *

They Said It Better Than Me

Life is not measured by the number of breaths we take, but by the moments that take our breath away.

—Vicki Corona,
ascribed to Maya Angelou

* * * * *

The journey is the reward.

—Tao Proverb

* * * * *

Strangers are **just family** you have **yet** to come to know.

—Mitch Albom

* * * * *

The true sign of intelligence is not knowledge but imagination.

—Albert Einstein

* * * * *

* * * * *

The best and most **beautiful things in the world cannot be seen or even touched—they must be felt with the heart."**

—Helen Keller

* * * * *

Success consists of **going from failure to failure without loss of enthusiasm.**

—Winston Churchill

* * * * *

Following Through and Perfect Practice

The more impatient you are, the more mistakes you are likely to make.

It's not how many times you get knocked down that counts, it is how many times you get back up.

* * * * *

Optimism is the key to success,
in everything.

* * * * *

See and feel what it is like to perfectly
execute a physical skill you desire
to achieve.

* * * * *

To enhance a physical skill, it is not practicing that counts. Rather it is only 'perfect practice' that will enable you to improve that skill.

* * * * *

* * * * *

Someone once said that to achieve success in anything, ninety percent consists in just showing up and ten percent consists of really busting your butt.

* * * * *

Compassion

* * * * *

It's Fun to Be Kind

* * * * *

It is better to be nice than
to be right.

* * * * *

Compassion toward others in need, should be your life's goal.

* * * * *

The simplest act of caring can turn a person's life around, forever.

* * * * *

Even though you may feel you are right about something, consider the possibility that you could be wrong.

* * * * *

The most beautiful people in the world that I have treated as a physician and psychologist, are those with a heart of gold, like Down's Syndrome children and adults.

✳ ✳ ✳ ✳ ✳

When something goes wrong between you and another person, try to figure out what could have been your contribution to the problem.

* * * * *

Be kind to those who have experienced PTSD. They have experienced tremendous horror. They will have pain and suffering from it every day of their life.

* * * * *

It is important to consider what is okay to good in your life and not to complain about what is not that important. Here are some examples.

* * * * *

Now Let Me Hear You Complain

A wounded warrior got off the plane from Afghanistan where both of his legs had been blown off by a mine. Now let me hear you complain that your brand-new shoes are a little bit too tight.

* * * * *

* * * * *

A young mother is sobbing hysterically as she has just been told that her three-year-old daughter has an inoperable brain tumor and that she will not survive for more than a few months. Now let me hear you complain that the co-pay on your daughter's health insurance just went up five dollars.

* * * * *

Today, fifteen thousand children around the world will die of starvation. Now let me hear you complain that you got shorted out of a full pack of French fries as you went thru the drive-thru at McDonalds today.

* * * * *

* * * * *

Many children cannot afford to pay for their books, paper, computers or I Pads. Now let me hear you complain that the cost of your favorite takeout food went up five dollars.

* * * * *

About fifty million Americans live in poverty. Now let me hear you complain that your 401k did not go up as much as you would have liked.

* * * * *

In a Pandemic, when around people, if you refuse to wear a mask or social distance, you might have oppositional/ defiant disorder. You are putting your health and your loved ones at risk for serious illness and death.

* * * * *

Gratefulness

Instead of complaining about things, make a list of things for which you are grateful.

* * * * *

Be grateful to those who give you an opportunity to participate in something special.

* * * * *

Be grateful to those who have contributed to your successes in life.

* * * * *

Regardless of the end, be grateful for the opportunity to love and be loved.

* * * * *

Inner Smile

We all must risk failure to
achieve success.

* * * * *

If you are complimented for having done something well, let them know that your success was due to the contribution of many people. Rather than, "I did it well," "We did it well."

* * * * *

Enjoy your "<u>inner smile</u>" when <u>you achieve</u> success in something that others said you were totally incapable of doing.

* * * * *

* * * * *

Enjoy your "<u>inner smile</u>" when you achieve success in something that <u>you realized</u> would be difficult and you persisted anyways.

* * * * *

Cranky

If you are cranky and critical, maybe it's because you really do not like yourself.

* * * * *

Try seeing the humor in everyone and everything. It will help make you be less of a grouch.

* * * * *

Finally

If you are cranky, no one is going to want to play with you.

* * * * *

We'd like to know if you enjoyed the book.
Please consider leaving a review on the platform from which you purchased the book

CPSIA information can be obtained at www.ICGtesting.com
Printed in the USA
BVIW122004021020
590212BV00001B/1